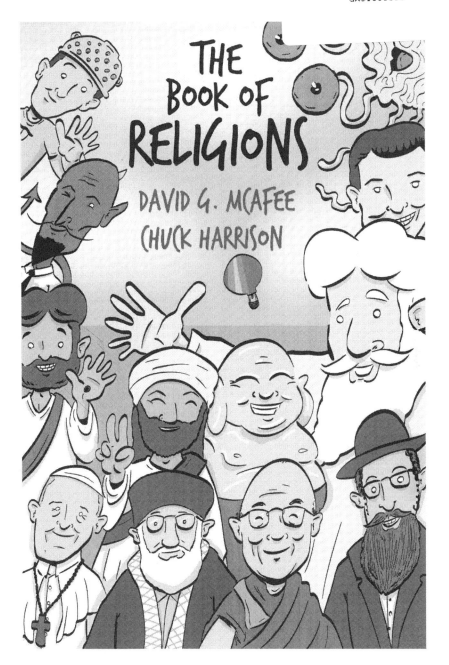

THE BOOK OF RELIGIONS

WRITTEN BY DAVID G. MCAFEE AND CHUCK HARRISON

WITH ILLUSTRATIONS BY CHUCK HARRISON

Published by Atheist Republic, an international nonprofit organization.

All rights reserved.

THE ATHEIST REPUBLIC

This book was published by Atheist Republic, a non-profit organization with upwards of a million fans and followers worldwide that is dedicated to offering a safe community for atheists around the world to share their ideas and meet like-minded individuals. Atheists are a global minority, and it's not always safe or comfortable for them to discuss their views in public.

At the very least, discussing one's atheistic views can be uncomfortable and ostracizing. In some countries, speaking out against religion can put someone in physical danger. By offering a safe community for atheists to share their opinions, Atheist Republic hopes to boost advocacy for those whose voices might otherwise be silenced.

All rights reserved.

No part of this publication may be reproduced, stored in or introduced into a retrieval system, or transmitted, in any form, or by any means (electronic, mechanical, photocopying recording or otherwise) without the prior written permission of the publisher.

Illustrations by Chuck Harrison and David G. McAfee

This book is sold subject to the condition that it shall not, by way of trade or otherwise, be lent, resold, hired out, or otherwise circulated without the publisher's prior consent in any form of binding or cover other than that in which it is published and without a similar condition including this condition being imposed on the subsequent purchaser.

KINDA BORING INTRO (FOR GROWN UPS)

The Book of Religions is the third in a series of books for kids of all ages on belief, gods, and religion. We've already learned about general beliefs and where they come from, and about the gods that are the subjects of some of those beliefs. So, on *this* stretch of the journey, we think it's important to discuss the religions – the belief *systems* – that are created when you combine the two.

For years we have condensed tough concepts surrounding faith and science to reading that is comfortable for children, and what we've found out is that kids often learn best via a step-by-step process that is both interactive and informative. Because of this, *The Book of Religions* is built upon information children would have gleaned from the first two books in the series. If your family doesn't yet have *The Belief Book* and *The Book of Gods*, we recommend picking those up before diving into this one.

That being said, regardless of where you stand on the religious spectrum, or what you've already read, we hope you enjoy the book… and maybe even learn something!
Never stop asking big
questions!

Your pals,
Dave and Chuck

David G. McAfee is a journalist and author of *No Sacred Cows: Investigating Myths, Cults, and the Supernatural*, among other works. He is also a frequent contributor to American Atheist Magazine. McAfee, who writes about science, skepticism, and faith for his *No Sacred Cows* blog on Patheos, attended University of California, Santa Barbara, and graduated with bachelor's degrees in English and Religious Studies with an emphasis on Christianity and Mediterranean religions.

I dedicate this book to my wife and final editor, Rachael, as well as my sister, Sharona, and her family. My niece and nephew, Alex and Hayden, were a huge inspiration when working on these books for kids. – David

Chuck Harrison is a writer and illustrator who lives with his son called Puff and his cat named Monkey in New York.

For the past 10 years his books, plays, comics, and illustrations have found their way around the globe. Mostly because of the internet, but also because some trees have been harmed. He feels really bad about the trees but not too bad to stop making books out of them.

I wish to dedicate this book as always to my favorite human on planet earth, my son and constant inspiration, Elijah but also to the Frazier and Humphrey Families. Spending time with all of you was instrumental in the creation of this book. – Chuck

CONTENTS

WELCOME TO THE BOOK OF RELIGIONS! 1
WHAT'S RELIGION? 4
THE WHY OF WORSHIP 8
THE HOW OF WORSHIP 14
RITUAL, RITUAL, RITUAL 21
RULES FROM ABOVE AND BELOW 27
SPECIAL STORY TIME 35
    CHRISTIAN BIBLE 37
    QUR'AN 38
    THE BOOK OF MORMON 39
    PRINCIPIA DISCORDIA 40
    BHAGAVAD GITA 41
RELIGIONS FROM AROUND THE WORLD! 46
    ISLAM 47
    HINDUISM 48
    BUDDHISM 49
    JUDAISM 50
    PASTAFARIANISM 51
    JAINISM 52
    SATANISM 53
    RAËLISM 55
    THE CHURCH OF THE SUBGENIUS 56
    BAHÁ'Í FAITH 57
LET'S PLAY FOLLOW THE PROPHET! 61
PLEASE RELIGION RESPONSIBLY 67
CONCLUSION 72
WRITING SPACE 76

WELCOME TO THE BOOK OF RELIGIONS!

Hello, and welcome to *The Book of Religions*! We're so happy that you're joining us on our latest voyage, which is part of a super awesome and important journey of knowledge and discovery!

It's a journey that started in *The Belief Book*, where we learned about what belief is, where it came from, and why it's so important to everyone. Then it continued in *The Book of Gods*, which taught us where gods came from and why some people worship them. We even created some gods of our own.

It's been an amazing trip, one that has led you here with this book in your hands.

By the time you're done reading it, you'll not only know just what religions are, you'll also have an idea of how they help shape the world we all live in – and even how they work!

So, are you ready to know just what religion is and how it's a part of your life even if you don't know it? Great! Let's strap on our thinking caps and go on an adventure of learning!

Wait a minute. How do we do that? Maybe we can learn all about religions by learning how to invent one of our own? Maybe the thinking caps can be a part of it?

That's just what we will do! As you begin the last part of this journey, you'll get to use what you've learned about belief and gods to create your own unique religion! Are you excited? So are we! Let's not waste another moment then. Let's start something new!

WHAT'S RELIGION?

At least once in your life, someone you know and trust has probably taken you to a building that was filled with people. You watched as the people sat and listened to one person (who may or may not be dressed funny) as they talked about things that sounded magical, things beyond what you can see, touch, hear, and feel. You might have noticed how the people listening did whatever the person speaking told them to do. This could be singing, or even standing up and then sitting down again. You probably had no idea what was going on. All you were told was that you were going to a place called *church* to pay respects to someone named "*God*".

But why? If you read *The Book of Gods* you got to learn that there have been thousands of "gods" ever since the first humans started making them up forever ago. So, why do these people go to "church" to worship just one of them? Wouldn't it just be easier to stay in bed and pay respects to their god in comfort? But no, they do not stay in bed, and the reason why is really simple: it's *religion*!

You probably got to go to a place where you had a first-hand experience with a religion, but that doesn't mean you knew all about what you were seeing. And knowing about things is awesome! So, what is religion, and why is it so important?

That's the question this book is going to answer! Why? Because we want to create a religion of our own and we don't really know what a religion is yet. We know what beliefs and gods are. So maybe there's something there. We know that people worship gods, but we're not quite sure of what that means. We need some answers and, to get those, we need to turn to one of Dave and Chuck's all-time favorite books: The dictionary!

The dictionary says this about **religion**:

Re·li·gion *[ri-lig-uhn]*

noun

1. A group of beliefs, ideas, and rules, sometimes related to belief in and worship of god(s), that can be used to help people be good or even to find meaning.

Dave and Chuck aren't religious, but they still love learning about different beliefs and where they came from.

After reading that, knowing what we know about belief and gods, religion doesn't seem as confusing as it once was!
"Religion" just means that there are people out there who believe in gods and try to follow their rules, right?

Well, not quite. It's a little more complicated than that. Mostly because when you have a religion that you follow, it's usually not *just* about belief in a god. It's way more than that! Our definition says, *'the belief in and worship of...'* That points our minds and tunes our thinking caps to a new direction of discovery!

We need to find out about worship if we want to really understand what a religion truly is! For this part of our journey, we have to learn not only what worship is, but *why* people love it so much. How are we supposed to do that?

That's a great question! Here's your answer:

Let's move on to Chapter Two to see what worship is all about!

THE WHY OF WORSHIP

Let's jump right into the meaning of **worship** with another piece from Dave and Chuck's favorite book, the dictionary!

Wor·ship *[wur-ship]*

noun

    1. To show honor or respect to a god, higher being, idea, or thing.

*Dave and Chuck don't **worship** anything because they don't have a religion and they don't believe in gods.*

That's super neat, but what does it *mean*? Well, we know that in ancient times (before there was even such a thing as a bed time) people made all sorts of little objects to represent the things they loved (or worshiped).

But their "gods" were different back then, and they worshiped things like water and the warm, light-giving sun. Can you think of anything you worship?

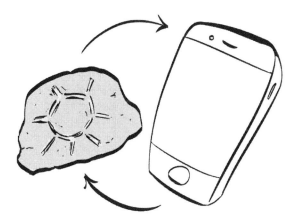

You may not worship your phone, but some people sure seem to! They stare at it and **interact** with it all the time.

In·ter·act *[in-ter-akt]*

verb

1. Talking to or dealing with something in a direct way.

*A lot of people who worship certain gods don't **interact** with Dave and Chuck and other non-believers because their Holy Books tell them not to.*

When we say people interact with their phones, we're saying they touch it and look at it. They laugh and cry at it. It's an object that seems to be really, really important to them. A thing they can't live without. Could a phone be a God? It hasn't happened yet, but with our imagination, anything is possible!

That brings us back to our journey of creating our own belief system! To start out, all you have to do is think of something you want to worship in your religion, or which God will make up the rules that form your faith.

Use this space to brainstorm about your religion, and what its followers will believe:

....
....
....
....
....
....
....
....
....
....
....
....
....

Have you invented your god yet? Have you thought of some rules you would like? You should because it's not only super fun, but also it will let us go on to the next part of our journey. To do that... we need a god or an idea to center our religion on!

Your god or idea that will be at the core of your religion can be anything you want it to be, anything you can think or imagine! Maybe you love the idea of having ice cream for breakfast. Why not invent a religion all about that? Look at your feet. Do you see any sneakers? Well, if you want, that shoe can be a god!

Now, love your GOD SNEAKER ⚡

– or whatever you chose – with all that is in you (or at least pretend that you do). Do you love it? Yes? Yes! You love your GOD SNEAKER ⚡ and now you're ready to start a religion all about worshiping it!

What if you didn't choose an object to worship? What if your idea isn't attached to anything at all? Well, that's okay. Using your imagination, you can create just about anything and, as long as you love it more than anything else, you're well on your way to creating a religion!

Here's a space for your god (or idea) to live in:

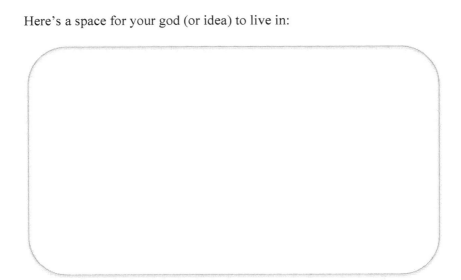

As long as you love your god or idea more than life itself, you should be set! But that's a whole lot of love for anything, isn't it? It sure is! So how could you ever possibly show something that much love? Let's move on to the next chapter to learn exactly how best to do it!

THE HOW OF WORSHIP

We've learned a lot so far! We now know that if we are going to create a religion of our own, we must have a god or idea that we can worship. We also know that worship is showing a god or idea more love than anything else in the whole wide world. But *how* do we show that love? What can we do to show something we love it more than anything else?

This seems like a huge task! So how about we take a look at some other religions from around the globe and see how they worship? Maybe we'll discover something fun or weird!

We've hopped over to the Middle East, where a lot of people practice a religion called Islam. Let's visit with a Muslim during their prayer time! They have to bow down like this and say words from their special book while facing their holy city about five times a day. Wow, that seems like a lot to do! They must really love their god to worship him like this.

Next, let's jump on over to the United States, where Christianity is the most popular religion. We see a follower of Jesus doing kind of the same thing as the follower of Muhammad and Allah, or a Muslim. Only the follower of Jesus Christ, or Christian, gets to pray whenever they want!

Some Christians also pray with deadly snakes, because they think their god will protect them. There's a sentence or two in their holy book that says snakes can't kill you if you love Jesus and they think it's totally true. Please don't do this yourself because you'll most likely not live to tell about it.

Many Christians also dunk babies in water! …wait. Why would you want to do that? How is that even worship?

To you and me it may look strange, but there's always a reason behind why and how people worship. In the case of the baby dunking, Christians believe that splashing some water on their head is a good way of showing their god that they don't like any other god except him. That's what people did in the Bible, so Christians do it now. It's called being *baptized*! Maybe you were once baptized, or your parents were.

Now we find ourselves on the continent of Asia. This is a Buddhist monk who is practicing something called "meditation." He sits quietly and in self-reflection thinking about the teachings from the Buddha, who started the religion known as Buddhism. We got to meet and learn all about him in *The Book of Gods*. This is like prayer in other religions, except the person focuses on themselves instead of gods. It's also pretty relaxing.

Maybe you can think of a way people should worship your god or idea? Here's a space below for you to write down some notes, and remember: they can be as wild as you'd like! Just keep in mind that worship is all about showing love and **devotion** to your deity.... how best to do that is all up to you!

De·vo·tion *[deh-voh-shun]*

noun

1. Love or loyalty for a person, activity, or cause.

*Dave and Chuck show **devotion** to their families and loved ones, but other people choose to devote their lives to gods who never interact with them.*

....
....
....
....
....
....

....
....
....
....
....
....
....
....
....

As you can see from some of the (hopefully fun and silly) things you've written, there is no wrong way to worship! As long as you are showing love for your god or your idea, you can worship any way you'd like. But be careful, because for some, the way you worship can be **habit** forming!

Hab·it *[hab-it]*

noun

    1. A regular practice that is hard to give up. A tradition.

*Dave and Chuck don't worship any deities, but they have other **habit**s! Dave likes to play video games, while Chuck enjoys drinking coffee every single morning!*

You may already have some habits yourself, like brushing your teeth before bed or kicking your shoes off your feet instead of untying them. Or, maybe you never brush your teeth before bed? Maybe you're always careful to untie your shoes before taking them off? If you do these things every day, they can become habits.

Can you think of any other habits you may have? We bet you can!

There are so many it would be hard to list them all. But did you know that something magical happens when you mix habit with religion? Do you want to find out what that is? All you have to do is take a look at chapter four!

RITUAL, RITUAL, RITUAL

Here's a short story…

A long, long time ago there was a man who thought the sun was a god. He worshiped his god by dancing in its warming rays every single day. One day the man did not dance and the next morning, when he woke up, the sun was hidden behind thick, dark clouds. He became so frightened that he danced and danced until the sun came back. After this, the man never missed another day of sun dancing for the rest of his life. His dance became a **ritual**, and here's what that means…

Rit·u·al *[rich-oo-uhl]*

noun

1. A special action done in the same way many times. A religious practice or tradition honored at certain times by some believers.

*Dave and Chuck think **ritual**s, which are more than just habits, are the most interesting parts of religions. But they can be dangerous, too. Some belief systems make people go without food for days at a time!*

From what we know about ancient religions and how they came to be, we know that many people started out worshiping nature, which is all the things outside your window not built by a human. The sun, moon, and Earth – as well as its trees and rocks and animals and just about anything that gave early humans something good – were all worshiped. Eventually that worship became a ritual and a habit, like in the story above about the man and the sun.

What was left out of the story was *how* the man danced, because over time that also changed. He changed his dance to better worship, or love, the sun. He even came up with a different dance that he believed could make it rain so his fruits and vegetables would grow.

Those changes eventually became part of the ritual! Every step of the dances took on great meaning and importance. If he missed a step of the dance, or messed one up, he was beyond sure there would be really bad **consequences** from the sun itself!

Con·se·quence *[kon-si-kwens]*

noun

1. Something that happens because of something else.

*Dave and Chuck know that sun and rain aren't **consequences** of any dance ritual, but they enjoy learning about the practice anyway!*

The man believed that, if he didn't dance, the food planted in the ground would not grow. Or that the sun would go away completely and leave the world in darkness! The fear of these things happening made it so the man *had* to dance. The dance was no longer filled with the love and joy it used to have. It became an act of worship out of fear, and it was repeated over and over again.

The fun and love were replaced with fear and endless rules! Rules about where he could put his feet and how he could move his body. Rules about what time of day he could dance and where he could boogie. Rules for the clothing he had to wear and what he could eat and drink before the dance. There were so many rules that it started to control the man's life!

Isn't it just enough to have a god or idea and to love it more than anything? So much so you dance for it to show that love? Isn't that what a religion is all about?

Yes, and no. On one hand, religion is about loving a god or idea, but on the other it's a whole set of rules about *how* to love that god or idea.

Want to know more about rules? …probably not. But the next chapter isn't all about learning rules, it's also about how to make some of your own!

RULES FROM ABOVE AND BELOW

And on that day at breakfast time the God of Ice Cream came out of his cotton candy cloud and handed down his rules, which were carved into stone tablets. The first rule was as follows: All beings shall have ice cream for breakfast every single day of the week and double ice cream for breakfast every Saturday, so says the God of Ice Cream! – Holy Book of ICG, Rocky Road, Chapter 7, Verse 42.

You see, to worship the God of Ice Cream the right way, you have to consume ice cream for breakfast every day with double servings on Saturdays. It's written down, so it must be true, right? Why would the God of Ice Cream lie to us? Doesn't he love us as much as we love him? Well, that's up to whoever is writing the thoughts and feelings of the God of Ice Cream.

Just like it will be up to you to decide just how someone will worship your god or idea. That's the fun of creating a religion! You get to be the one in charge for a change!

Don't like the idea of homework or bedtimes? Don't like having to take tests or having to clean your room? Well, you'll never have to do any of those things again if you invent a god or idea that says you don't have to.

You can claim that it's against your religion! Of course, you might learn that your parents or loved ones don't share your religious views.

But before we get to the good things about religion, let's talk about the rules. Basically, religions are all about rules. How do you worship a god? What do you have to do to go to heaven? How many pieces of silver do you have to pay if you steal your neighbor's donkey?

That last one might not matter anymore unless your neighbors have a donkey. But, sadly they probably do not, so that rule seems like it's better for the past rather than for now. You'll see that a lot if you decide to learn about different religions, and you definitely should since you're making one of your own!

Here's an awesome start: In the Bible, the holy book for the most popular religion in the world (Christianity), there are rules for how to cut your hair!

Leviticus 19:27: *"Do not cut the hair at the sides of your head or clip off the edges of your beard."*

Every religion has rules, and for very important reasons! Without them, how would anyone know how to follow any religion? What would the people who want to follow a religion do to show love and devotion to their god?

A religion without rules would be total chaos! You've spent all this time coming up with your god or idea and how to worship it, so shouldn't you protect it? You can with a shield of rules! A mighty shield that will stop people from changing and messing with your creation!

To do this, we're going to have to sit down and come up with a list rules for our new religion. Your rules can be as simple as a special word your followers must say, like how Christians have to say *"Amen"* after they pray while Pastafarians say *"R'Amen"*.

If you're not sure what a Pastafarian is, let us explain. That's someone who practices Pastafarianism, which is a made-up religion all about the Flying Spaghetti Monster, and the number one rule is that the FSM does not exist. It's also considered very polite to wear a strainer, or colander, on your head. That's the thing you put in the sink to get the water out of the spaghetti or to clean the yucky dirt off those very tasty vegetables!

Wait, maybe it's tasty dirt off of yucky vegetables? Hmmm...

You can make fun rules like in Pastafarianism yourself! You can also make your rules super **complex** like the ones found in Judaism, Hinduism, and even some branches of Christianity.

Com·plex *[kom-pleks]*

adjective

1. Complicated or having many moving parts.

*Dave and Chuck know some religious rituals and traditions have **complex** pieces, such as dangerous consequences if they are not performed the right way.*

It's very important to think of why you're making these rules up. In most branches of Christianity, members are supposed to tell people about

Jesus. That's one of their main rules. Why? Because it helps the religion to spread and gain more followers. So, do your rules have a real reason?

Another thing to think about: is this a rule from your god or yourself (the prophet of that god)? In the religion of Islam, the prophet Muhammad made up rules he said came from his god, Allah. In the Old Testament of the Bible, God comes to Earth as a burning bush to give Moses his laws. We have many options, but interesting stories work better!

You can make up whatever you want, as long as every rule you make tells us *why* and *how* you think people should love your god (or how your god demands people love it).

Most importantly, have fun with them! Maybe you have a rule that everyone in your religion has to smile at least once a day, or that everyone has to have ice cream for breakfast. The choice is yours!

Here's some space for your own rules:

....
....
....
....
....
....
....
....
....
....
....
....
....
....
....

Don't worry if you ran out of room to write your rules down here. We know you may have a bunch, which is why you'll find additional blank pages to write and draw on in the back of this book. Once you have your rules written down, please join us in chapter six for a special surprise!

SPECIAL STORY TIME

Surprise! It's special story time. And the story we're going to be talking about today is locked inside your brain right now. It's the story of your religion! But you probably think that a story is just a story, right? Well, you'd be right, but also a little bit wrong…

You wouldn't hurt someone over your favorite comic book or cartoon show, would you? Well, for some people, religious stories are really extra special. They are so special that they become more than just fun ways to pass the time; they can become something called **sacred**, something to kill (or die) for!

Sa·cred *[sey-krid]*

Adjective

1. Something with special religious meaning; an idea that can't be questioned.

*Dave and Chuck don't have any complex religious beliefs, but they think coffee is a **sacred** drink.*

Now it's your turn to write a text based on your religion! This is something that may take you a while, but to help get you started, here are a few things to think about putting in your religious text (also called a *Holy Book*):

- A story or stories about how the world was created.
- Lessons on how people should act.
- Directions on how to worship your deity or idea.
- Possibly something evil for your followers to fear and your god to fight against.

This seems like a big task, doesn't it? It is, but you don't have to worry! So many other people before you have already done it, so you'll have some help. To get a better idea of what to do, let's take a closer look at some of the most popular religious reads on the planet:

CHRISTIAN BIBLE

The Christian Bible is made up of two "testaments," called Old and New. The Old Testament is also used by Jewish people, and even Muslims. It contains stories about the creation of the world and how early Jews were supposed to act. The New Testament, only found in Christianity, has stories about Jesus, who believers say was Yahweh's (God's) son. In that book, Jesus, who believers say is both human and god, was born to the virgin Mary. He also brings himself back to life after being killed on a cross!

QUR'AN

The Qur'an, the Holy Book of Islam, is a sister to the Christian Bible and another child of the Jewish writings. The Prophet Muḥammad said he inspired the Qur'an after being contacted by God through an angel named Gabriel. According to one story from the Qur'an, Muḥammad flew to heaven on a white horse with wings!

THE BOOK OF MORMON

Mormons, members of the Church of Latter Day Saints, believe the Book of Mormon is a newer new testament of Christianity. The Book of Mormon was written by Joseph Smith, the prophet of the Mormon religion, and it describes ancient people who they think lived in the United States before Native Americans. Believers say the sacred text was written on golden plates that were shown to Smith by an angel, kind of like Muhammad and the Qur'an!

PRINCIPIA DISCORDIA

Principia Discordia is the holy text of Discordianism, a religion in which believers worship a goddess called Eris. Discordians believe the world is confusing and that order isn't real, so they focus on not taking life too seriously. In fact, the five rules of Discordianism (called the *Pentabarf*... yes, really) include a rule that believers must go enjoy a hot dog alone on a Friday.

BHAGAVAD GITA

The Bhagavad Gita, sometimes just called The Gita, is just one of the many sacred books in Hinduism. The Gita teaches people to act **selflessly**.

Self·less *[self-lis]*

adjective

1. Not thinking of yourself; the opposite of selfish.

*Dave and Chuck don't believe The Gita is sacred, but they still agree that people should act **selflessly** by putting other people before themselves.*

The Gita also has a story about Arjuna, a prince and warrior in doubt about his choices, and his guide who is also a form of God.

As you see, holy books are just stories… but to many people they are really special stories also known as **teachings**.

Teach·ing *[tee-ching]*

noun

1. Ideas taught by a teacher, or somebody in a position of authority.

*Dave and Chuck value important **teachings** in different religions, such as the Hindu idea of selflessness, without being religious.*

Are you ready to write down your religious teachings? This is where you get to tell people about your god or idea and your rules, as well as any

fun stories you came up with along the way! Jesus, the lead prophet and kind of god of Christianity, liked to tell stories called **parables** that other people wrote down many years after his death.

Par·a·ble *[par-uh-buh l]*

noun

1. A short story that has a deeper meaning or religious idea.

*Dave and Chuck think the best way to spread any good teachings is through catchy **parables** that tell an important story in a simple way.*

Jesus liked to use parables to spread his religious beliefs, but Muhammad, the prophet of Islam, liked to go into a cave all by himself to make up his teachings.

You don't have to go into a cave, because your bedroom will be just fine. Here's a small space to write your Holy Book. You'll probably need a lot more if you let your imagination run wild!

....
....
....
....
....
....
....
....

....
....
....
....

You may have only written down a little bit of your sacred story, but don't worry, there's a lot more space in the back of this book so you can keep writing if you still need to! Eventually you can just get your own notebook, as this is recommended for a realistic and complete religion.

But what does a real, complete religion even look like? Would you like to see some examples? Awesome! Pack your bag and step inside our wonderful, world-traveling magic balloon because we're going on a trip around the world!

RELIGIONS FROM AROUND THE WORLD!

You've come a long way on your quest to learn all about religion, and even to create your own! Now, imagine you're in a balloon soaring above the earth. As you look down, you're able to see all of Earth's people (7 billion and counting!) as well as the thousands and thousands of religions they invent and practice. Let's fly over and take a look at some of the strangest and most popular ones!

ISLAM

We'll start with the second most popular and fastest- growing religion on the planet, Islam, a close relative to Christianity and another Judaism. Islam is based on the teachings of its founder, Muḥa[mmad, who] believers (called Muslims) say was sent by God to help people. Muslims believe the purpose of life is to worship God, or "Allah," and to give to charity without other people knowing (zakat). They also have strict rules against drawing their leader. In fact, some people have been killed just for making a cartoon of Muḥammad. Here's a picture of the Muslim prophet Muhammad, but because no one is allowed to draw him we really don't know what he looks like. It's a total mystery!

HINDUISM

Next is Hinduism, which is the third-largest religion in the world, and one of the oldest that is still being practiced  today. There are about a billion Hindus in the world, and many of them are in India. Hindus fall into three main groups: Vaishnavism, which holds Vishnu to be the most important god, Shaivism, which focuses on Shiva, and Shaktism, in which believers mostly worship Devi. Most Hindus believe in reincarnation, which means every living person or animal is reborn after death as a different being.

BUDDHISM

Now, let's take a look at the fourth-largest religion, Buddhism, a branch of Hinduism founded by Gautama Buddha. There are more than 500 million Buddhists in the world, and many of them believe in reincarnation just like the Hindus! Most Buddhists practice the "Noble Eightfold Path" and hope to one day escape the ongoing rebirth they believe we all face. Many of you probably think of Buddhists as the always peaceful people, but many of them have used violence in the name of their religion.

JUDAISM

And we can't forget about Judaism, which isn't the biggest religion, but it's still really important! Without Judaism, we wouldn't have Christianity OR Islam!  Both of those religions are based on the Hebrew stories of Yahweh, Abraham, and Moses found in the Torah, which actually makes up the first five books of the Old Testament of the Christian Holy Bible. Jews, who call themselves the "Chosen People," believe that God has a special relationship with their entire group!

PASTAFARIANISM

Those were fun, but we can have more fun by going to outer space in our magic hot air balloon to check out Pastafarianism, AKA the Church of the Flying Spaghetti Monster (FSM).  This is a religion that was made by someone like you in 2005! The yummy spaghetti monster god was created to make a point about not teaching religious ideas in science classes. FSM may have started out as a joke, but Pastafarianism is now a legally recognized religion in some countries!

JAINISM

Back to Earth and scouting the horizon for our next religion... there it is: Jainism! You probably haven't heard of Jainism, but it's known as the most peaceful religion ever! Jainism is a really old religion that came from Hinduism.

It isn't practiced much today, but it's still super cool because Jains don't believe in hurting anyone or anything. They don't even eat animals! In fact, some Jains carry around little brooms with them everywhere they go so that they don't kill any little bugs as they walk! As crazy as it sounds, even some Jains have used violence to push their non-violent ideas, proving all religions can be bad when taken to extremes.

SATANISM

Wait a minute… what's that directly below us? It's Satanism! Cool, let's check it out! Satan is a really bad guy in Christianity and Islam, so most people think "Satanists" are evil, but that's not  really true. Most Satanists don't even believe in Satan or God! Satanism is based on the character of Satan, but that character is seen as a **symbol** for knowledge or truth to them.

Sym·bol *[sim-buh l]*

noun

1. An idea that means something else; a representation.

*Dave and Chuck know **symbols**, such as a Christian cross, are strong enough to cause happiness as well as violence!*

Satanists are often attacked by Christians and other groups, but Satanism today focuses on the natural world, asking questions, and being kind to people who deserve it. The Church of Satan has 11 Satanic Rules, including, "Do not harm little children," and members who attend services all around the world. All that without any magical beliefs!

RAËLISM

Oh, no! Our balloon is getting beamed up by Raëlism! That's one of the most popular "UFO religions," which all say that alien beings created or control people on Earth.

The religion was founded in 1974, and today there are about 90,000 Raëlians in more than 90 countries who believe that aliens created humans as a type of lab experiment. This group also uses mixed racial and religious symbols, like a swastika combined with the Jewish Star of David. Their founder says he saw that image on an alien spaceship. Other UFO religions are Scientology and Heaven's Gate!

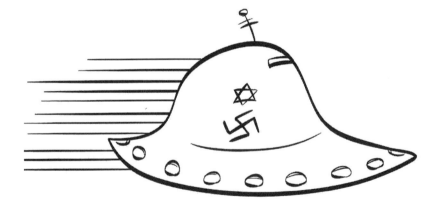

THE CHURCH OF THE SUBGENIUS

Let's get away from those ancient religions and aliens, and seek shelter in The Church of The SubGenius. It's a silly religion that makes fun of other religions by teaching a 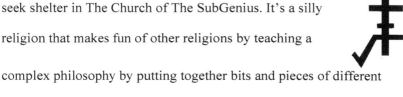 complex philosophy by putting together bits and pieces of different belief systems. Basically, it's like Scientology and Christianity, with UFO teachings and TV ads. There are about 40,000 members. Their main god, JHVH-1, or Jehovah 1, is a god made up of many other gods. The head prophet of the church, J.R. "Bob" Dobbs, is a

salesman from the 1950s whose face still appears on nearly all of the writings released by the church or its followers even today!

BAHÁ'Í FAITH

We're almost to our last stop, so let's bring it all together with The Bahá'í Faith! Those who practice this religion are all about all people uniting under one God. They believe in one God that created everything

and that each different religion comes from that God. That God is said to be all-powerful, all-loving, and too great for humans to even understand. Followers of Bahá'í are taught to focus on prayer and helping other people.

And, as we end our journey, we saved the best religion for last: yours!

What do you call your religion?

....

What's the symbol for your religion?

What's your religion all about?

Wow! That was a lot, and it was a really small percentage of the religions that are out there. Some experts say that there are thousands of new ones created every single day, including yours!

And there you are, listed with the heavy hitters. You've done a lot of hard work to invent your own religion, just like the other prophets, and you should be proud of your accomplishment! So, what now?

Now, you get to learn how to proselytize! What's that? How do you even say that? What does it mean? Read on to find out!

LET'S PLAY FOLLOW THE PROPHET!

By now, you should have your very own deity or idea as the basis of your new religion. You should also have a reason to worship the Creator you Created, and a set of rules that outline just how to do it. You may have also started writing your own holy book based on your religion. Do you know what this means?

It means you now have the beginnings of a religion that's all your own! All religions started just how yours did, with an idea someone loved, a set of rules on how to love it, and a story to help them teach and lead others. How cool is that?!

Do you know what else this means? It means you are a *prophet*. We learned a little bit about prophets in *The Book of Gods*, but here's a refresher: a prophet is a person who is said to bring a message from, or speak for, a god. Muhammad is a prophet of Islam, and Joseph Smith is the prophet of a religion even more closely related to Christianity called Mormonism. They are prophets because they claim to speak for a deity. Now, you get to do that too!

Wow! We're honored someone like you is even reading this book. You're so holy and wonderful. Every word from your lips is like hearing the voice of God! Your writings will be followed to the letter for all of

eternity! No one can say you're wrong because you hear the direct voice of God and speak for it! ...Is that how this works?

Now, you get to be the inspired teacher! You get to go out into the world and tell people all about what your god or idea can do for them. The people you tell can decide if your religion is the right one for them.

To get a better idea of how to do this, we'll go back in time and look at the creation of one of the world's most popular religions: Christianity! Before it was a massive religion, Christianity (and every other religion that was or ever will be) started as a **cult**.

Cult *[cult]*

noun

1. A small group of people who have a similar belief system, often controlled by a powerful leader.

*Dave and Chuck have studied enough history to know that **cult** leaders use all sorts of symbols and stories to create their religious groups.*

Saying that Christianity was once a cult isn't an insult. Not at all! It's simply a fact, like how at one point you were a little tiny baby. Another fact is that, right now, your religion is a small cult that may have you as its only member. But that can change! Christianity was a small cult that came out of Judaism thousands of years ago, and one of the first things that helped it become more than just a cult was something called **proselytization**.

Pros·e·lyt·ize *[pros-uh-li-tahyz]*
verb

1. To try to get someone to join your religion.

*Dave and Chuck love talking to religious **proselytizers** who go door-to-door trying to convince people to join their cult.*

Proselytization is very common in many religions. This is because it helps little cults grow up to be big and strong religions! Any time you tell someone all the good things about your religion, you're proselytizing and hopefully getting new members. But how can you do this?

Well, you could always wear a tie and go door to door like Mormons do. You could also just tell the people around you about it. Or you can even go to our Instagram page, @Bookofreligions, and post about it for us to see and read (be sure to ask your parents or guardian first before you do this!). Basically, whenever you open your mouth and talk about your religion with someone in order to get them to follow you, you're doing it right!

Now it's looking like you're all set to start this religion and prophet thing for real! Pretty soon you can start holding playground meetings and spreading the faith you made up yourself as far and wide as it can go, as long as it is safe and appropriate for school. In fact, you get bonus points if your religion can actually *help* all people! That would be an awesome religion!

But there is one last thing before you go out and tell everyone about the religion you just invented. It's a warning of sorts about exactly what not to do, while also being a way of showing what good you could do. Weird, right?

PLEASE RELIGION RESPONSIBLY

Religion has been with humanity for a long, long time. In that time, many religions have come and gone while some have stayed around in one form or another. Religion has been a powerful force on planet Earth. So powerful that people base their whole lives on just one book! Because of that, entire cities, cultures, and **societies** have built themselves up around one religion or another.

So·ci·e·ty *[suh-sahy-i-tee] noun*

1. A large group of people linked together by a community, sometimes by religion or country.

*Dave and Chuck know there are all types of people in our **society**, including those who proselytize their religion whenever they can.*

When we stop to think about the power religion still has in our society today, we can't help but notice how many people have suffered thanks to extremist followers. An extremist follower is someone who will hurt people or themselves in order to follow the holy book of their religion to the letter. Most of them have been brainwashed to believe they have to.

We learned in *The Belief Book* the importance of respecting someone else's beliefs, even if we disagree with them, while in *The Book of Gods* we learned how to become a Higher Power Ranger. We hope that by learning and understanding this, and making your religion a positive one, it will help humankind instead of hurting it.

Christianity, Islam, Judaism, Hinduism, and even Buddhism all have some very, very bad skeletons in their closets. Countless people of all ages have been put in prison for life, or even killed, just because they wouldn't believe in a certain religion, or they chose to believe and practice it differently.

Religious leaders have used their positions of respect in people's lives to control them in very bad ways, like having them kill other people or to reject their friends and family. They've also stolen from the people they've had killed for not believing, or even just questioning if their religion is true.

The whole world has been hurt because bad people with bad ideas have used nearly every religion as a weapon. Even people with good ideas have ended up doing bad things, like cutting family members out of their lives or trying to force others to live like them.

So, all you prophets have a big responsibility here. You don't want your religion used for evil! You want it to be used for good. And the religions mentioned above have done some truly amazing and wonderful things.

Science, math, medicine, art, and even the book you're holding all have something to do with religions. Isaac Newton, the scientist who discovered gravity and the laws of motion, was a very strict Christian his entire life. His religion guided him, and was not only a key part of his life, but also very important to his scientific and mathematic discoveries!

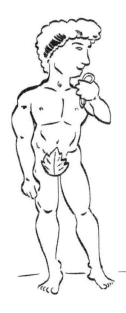
Many of the most famous works of art were paid for by the churches of different religions, or their rich followers, or inspired by someone's faith. Those amazingly awesome pieces have in turn inspired countless artists who have gone on to create everything from your favorite cartoons and video games to the drawings in this book, a book that is only here because Mr. Gutenberg invented the printing press around 1440. And the first major book to print was… the Christian Bible! The printed word would go on to be the biggest step to make communication between humans easier, until the internet.

Without all these things in your life, which were consequences of religion in some way or another, it would feel a whole lot emptier. So, religion has definitely made the world a much brighter place, as well as making it a darker one. You should create a religion of brightness. A religion about love that actually is about love, and not about money, power, control, or death. With less of that and more love, just imagine what a world it would be!

Conclusion

Well, here we are at the end of our voyage. It started with learning all about beliefs and gods, and is ending with a brand-new religion made by you. That's so incredible! You should feel a sense of pride for taking this journey. There are so many people in the world, even people who live right near you, who would be too afraid to take on this important task themselves.

It can be scary to learn new things, especially the stuff that goes against the way you're most comfortable seeing the world. But you beat that fear and now you have the knowledge of what a religion is (and maybe even the start of your own) to show for it! That's got to be one of the neatest things you've ever done. At least, to us it is!

Right now, your idea for a religion is like a little seed that needs all the right stuff so that it can sprout and grow into a big plant. With plenty of water and sunlight, and lots of care, who knows what will grow? It could be something beyond your wildest dreams! You could even change the world for the better.

Hopefully, this book helped you to not only understand what a religion is, but also *how a religion works*. And knowing how something works is just about one of the best ways you can understand it.

You have so much knowledge all about beliefs, gods, and religion in your head, it wouldn't be surprising if your brain grew twice the size!

Maybe you should put this book down for a second and check to see if your head has grown in size. We'll wait right here!

Has it?

Phew! That was a close one! Actually, no one in human history has ever had their brain get bigger just because they've learned too much. Well, no one that we know of. Maybe you could be the first?

All joking aside, you've come a long way and it's time to celebrate and share your new knowledge about religion with the world. You can do

this either by sharing what you've learned from this book, or by sharing your own religion.

We can't thank you enough for reading this series of books! It was really fun to create and share them with you. We hope you had as much fun reading them, and learning while creating a religion of your own. We can't wait to see what you all came up with!

We just hope your religion is one that says you can have ice cream for breakfast.

ADDITIONAL WRITING SPACE

Here's some additional creative spaces in case you needed more room to finish your religion (or start a new one)!

....
....
....
....
....
....
....
....
....
....
....
....
....
....
....

....
....
....
....
....
....
....
....

Printed in Great Britain
by Amazon